Japanese Movie Billboards
Retro Art from a Century of Cinema

CONTENTS

Introduction ● 4

**Part 1
Making a Movie Billboard** 7

The Making Of ● 8

**Part 2
Japanese Movie Billboards** 11

Roman Holiday ● 12
Casablanca ● 13
The Bodyguard ● 14
Musashi Miyamoto ● 15
Shane ● 16
Gone with The Wind ● 17
Purple Hood ● 18
New Tales from Many Lands　The Flute Playing Boy ● 19
The Seven Samurai ● 20
Charlie Chaplin in "Police" ● 20
Hanabi ● 21
Crimson Wings ● 22
The Storm Summoner ● 22
Bonnie and Clyde ● 23
Arch of Triumph ● 24
September Affair ● 25
Happiness and Pain and the Passing of Time ● 26
Pepe Le Moko ● 27
The Town with the Cupola ● 28
La Strada ● 30
Hibari, Chiemi and Izumi are the Three Sisters ● 31
Plein Soleil ● 32

Crimson Pistol ● 33
The Man with No Tomorrow ● 33
Breakfast at Tiffany's ● 34
The Red Peony Gambler　Oryu Comes Calling ● 36
Tangesazen the One-armed, One-eyed Ronin　The Enchanted Sword "Wet Swallow" ● 37
On the Waterfront ● 38
Romeo & Juliet ● 39
Some Like it Hot ● 40
Goodbye Milky Way Railroad 999 ● 41
The Flavour of Pike ● 42
Wheat Harvest ● 42
Love Story ● 43
The Notorious Port ● 44
Stagecoach ● 45
The Kid ● 46
Epic Poem ● 47
The Sound of Music ● 48
She Wore a Yellow Ribbon ● 50
The Summer of the Eclipse ● 51
The Bridge on the River Kwai ● 52
The Undefeated ● 53
Zatoichi The Blind Swordsman Nidangiri ● 54
Teenaged President ● 55
Princess Mononoke ● 56
Be Forever Yamato ● 56
Shinsengumi ● 57
Tales of Eight Dogs　The Monsters' Ball ● 58
High Noon ● 59
It's Tough to be a Man　The Talk about Torajirou ● 60
It's Tough to be a Man　Torajirou's Forget-me-not Grass ● 61
It's Tough to be a Man　Torajirou on the Path of Truth ● 61
It's Tough to be a Man　Torajirou is Lovesick ● 61
Pacific Porters ● 62
Himeyuri's Tower ● 63

Chisum ● 64
The Enemy Below ● 65
Senhime ● 66
New Tales from Many Lands The Red Peacock ● 67
Texas Across the River ● 68
Le Notti Di Cabiria ● 69
The Kurama Goblin The Wandering Child Acrobats ● 70
The Big Boss ● 71
Dangerous G-Men The Beast of the Underworld ● 72
The Man Who Crossed Hell ● 73
Lawrence of Arabia ● 74
The Naked Edge ● 76
Nonchan Rides the Clouds ● 77
Lonely Iyami in the Wind ● 78
Momotarou, the Musical ● 79
West Side Story ● 80
The Third Man ● 81
Your Name Is … Part 3 ● 82
Abashiri Special Zone Showdown in the South ● 83
Darling Clementine ● 84
Jeux Interdits ● 85
Daibosatsu Ridge Part 2 ● 86
Daibosatsu Ridge The Kougen Swordsmen ● 87
Daibosatsu Ridge The Epilogue ● 87
Floral Phoenix ● 88
Nakanori, the Bloody Fool! ● 89
Tarzan Escapes ● 90
City Lights ● 91
The Great Escape ● 92
The Foghorn Calls to Me ● 93

A short biography of Bankan Kubo ● 94
Movie Billboard Museum・Showa Magic Lantern Hall ● 94
INDEX ● 95

Japanese Movie Billboards

cocoro books

Published by DH Publishing, Inc.
1-20-2-518 Higashi-Ikebukuro, Toshima-ku
Tokyo 170-0013 Japan

www.dhp-online.com

cocoro books is an imprint of DH Publishing, Inc.

First Published 2008

Text and illustrations ©2008 by DH Publishing, Inc.

Printed in China
Printed by Miyuki Inter-Media Hong Kong, Inc.
Publisher: Hiroshi Yokoi
Editor: Youichi Toyoshima
Photographer: Takeshi Kubo and Junichi Kiyomiya
Designer: Naohiko Sasaki
Translator: Joe Greenholtz
ISBN: 978-1-932897-28-9

All rights reserved. No part of this publication may be reproduced, stored in a retrieval system, or transmitted in any form or by any means, electronic, mechanical, photocopying, recording or otherwise without the written consent of the publisher.

The Man Behind the Billboard

By Brett Bull

The inside of the JR train station in the city of Ome provides the first indication that there is something very unique about this sleepy Tokyo suburb at the edge of the Tama River.

On the platform, a staid John Wayne, cowboy hat firmly planted atop his head, stares at departing and arriving passengers from a billboard for the film "Stagecoach." Then there is Audrey Hepburn, black sunglasses dangling from her mouth in "Breakfast at Tiffany's," waiting inside the tunnel that leads to the ticket gate.

Outside, and throughout the city's streets, the fronts of many shops and restaurants feature yet more ominous imagery of screen heroes past, each brimming with vibrant colors and action: Humphrey Bogart and Ingrid Bergman embrace in "Casablanca" and Toshiro Mifune wields his sword in Akira Kurosawa's samurai flick "Yojimbo."

The man behind this nostalgic cinema tour is perhaps Japan's last remaining painter of old-style film billboards, Noboru Kubo.

"The reason I do the old movies is because I like the retro look," explains Kubo, who in 1941 was born in Ome, about one hour by train from Shinjuku. "Today's movies seem to be too detached from the feeling I want to express."

The first name on Kubo's business card reads "Bankan," a playful pronunciation twist on *kanban*, or billboard, and for much of his five decades in the business he has been postponing that inevitable day when this craft's last drop of paint hits the board.

His cramped studio is filled with blank veneer boards leaning on their edges. Tattered and creased film posters, primarily from his favorite genre, *chanbara* (sword-fighting), are plastered to the walls and strewn about the tables. Kubo always works in a bandana and sandals. The floor beneath his chair is splattered in specks and drips of color. To either side of him are buckets of paint with wood mixing sticks resting inside.

Kubo's work starts with a pencil, which is used to carefully make an outline of the main stars–for example, Marilyn Monroe's distinctive curves and low neckline in "Some Like it Hot." The mangled posters serve as guides for ensuring that each character's likeness and clothing style are replicated properly. "Of course I want to emphasize the main characters," he says of each billboard's layout. "But as well, I want to make it seem as if the characters are going to move as soon as you see them. I want the picture to seem dynamic, as if it is alive."

In his rendering for "Shichinin no Samurai," the hero, once again Mifune, legs astride and mouth about to let forth with a scream, swings his sword high above his head. For "Bonnie and Clyde," Warren Beatty grips the getaway car's steering wheel from behind its bullet-hole-filled windshield as Faye Dunaway slightly tilts her head and laughs.

Colors are applied so that the background scene, perhaps the airplane lifting from the runway in "Casablanca," appropriately blends with the larger characters. "There is no plan," Kubo says of his approach. "I just go with my instinct. All of the ideas pop into my head so I have no idea what I am doing from the start."

The billboards are not without their quirks. Audrey Hepburn appears to be absolutely disillusioned as she peers from a near ninety-degree rotation of her head in "Roman Holiday." Equally zombie-like is Alida Valli's blank stare past Orson Welles in "The Third Man."

Kubo's beginnings with the brush go back to when he was 13, a time when he frequently saw billboards posted in front of a theater near his house in Ome. One in particular that caught his eye was for a film starring Denjiro Okochi as the fictional character Tange Sazen, a one-eyed and one-armed samurai. "It was so catchy, so very impressive," Kubo recalls of that billboard.

From that point, he started drawing characters and pictures of his own in a notebook. Then after a six-month apprenticeship at an advertising company, where much of his work included washing dishes and sweeping floors, he approached a theater with samples of his work to request a job painting the billboards for nothing but the cost of the paints and brushes. By the age of 19, he was responsible for furnishing billboards for the three theaters in Ome.

Speed was of the essence. On average Kubo completed one billboard a day, but during the peak season, when three films might be screened at each theater in a week, his pace had to be upped.

While now many might see his work as a form of entertainment, in those days the works were strictly for functional purposes. "They were up for a week and then we stripped them down in favor of announcing the next feature," Kubo explains.

During the golden age of Japanese cinema in the 1950s and '60s, a time when legends like Kenji Mizoguchi, Yasujiro Ozu, and Kurosawa directed some of Japan's classic films, the number of screens swelled to over 7,000. But the popularity of television forced many to shut—by 1970, only 3,000 were in operation. For Kubo, this meant he had to find other work in Ome, whose last theater closed its doors in 1973. "When I was young, I dreamed of working at a big theater in the center of the city," he says. "But I had to give up hope when I became obsolete."

He turned to painting political posters, festival signs and funeral curtains. But when he found himself yearning for the films of his youth, Kubo started painting the retro billboards again. Following an art festival in Ome in 1993, various shopkeepers discovered that Kubo's billboards made for a nice tourist draw when mounted outside their buildings.

Today his pace has slowed to where each piece might take a week. He receives approximately 30 orders a year, with various painting work on the side taking up the remainder of his time.

While modern film billboard-makers use computers to create posters in a mass-produced fashion, the methods used by Kubo, who estimates he has produced over 3,000 billboards in his career, have remained largely unchanged. The only item powered by electricity in his studio is the lighting. For paint, such natural materials as seashells and charcoal are crushed and powdered to form his five basic colors—red, yellow, blue, white and black. Dubbed *doroenogu*, these natural pigments are held together by a binding element (*nikawa*) which is a paste formed from an extract of boiled animal and whale bones.

This traditional style of painting, which was commonly used in the Edo Period (1603-1868), results in colors that nearly jump from the board. But since the paint is organic and most of Ome's billboards are exposed to the elements, the sharpness is not everlasting. Rain and sunlight cause discoloration and fading. The non-permanence inherent in the work is a problem, too, in encouraging younger generations to take up the craft.

"Modern Japan is creative enough," Kubo says, "but it is extremely difficult to get people interested in painting with such rudimentary materials. So many young students go to universities where they make graphics on fancy computers."

First and foremost, Kubo's passion lies in an appreciation for films from a different era. Beyond that, he is reluctant to comment on his work.

"I would not say that this is art," he says. "I am a just professional who happens to be able to paint slightly better than the average person. So I'll let the public decide whether or not to call my work art."

As with many things in life, Kubo thinks that true appreciation will come once it is gone.

"I believe that in 100 years nobody will be doing this," he says. "It will be then that people will come around to realize just how valuable it is."

> Brett Bull is a Tokyo-based freelance writer who covers film for Variety and the Japan Times. He also writes the online column Sake-Drenched Postcards (http://www.bigempire.com/sake/).

Japanese Movie Billboards
What to Look For

Cast

Director

Star

Title

Catch copy

Roman Holiday ——————————————————————— (1)
It will give you goose bumps! The year's most talked about romantic movie. ——— (2)
U.S.A / 1953 / William Wyler

(3)　(4)　(5)

(1) Japanese title
(2) Catch copy
(3) Country of production
(4) Year of release
(5) Director

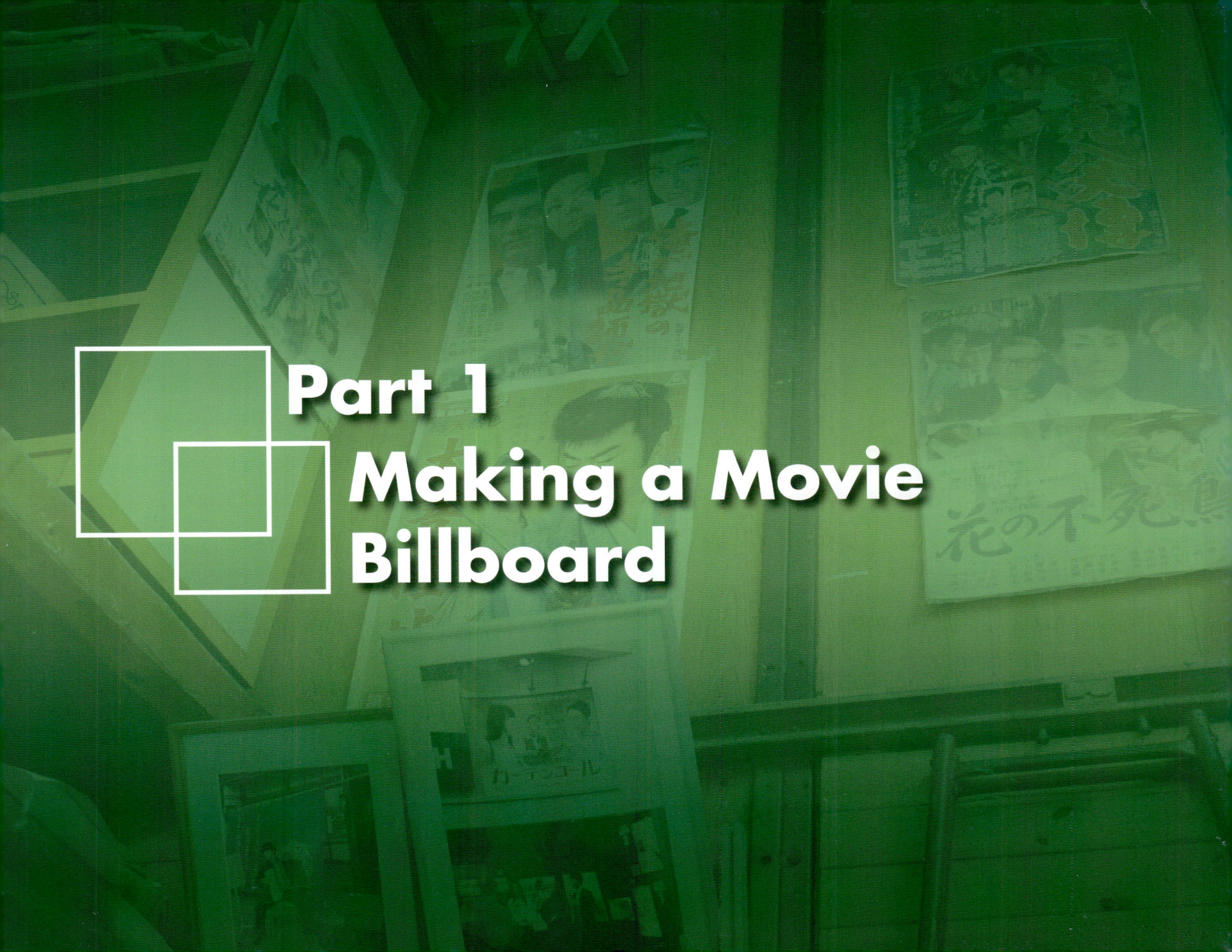

Part 1
Making a Movie Billboard

The Making Of

Billboard artist Bankan-san, who made the billboards in this book, explains how he works.

1 The first step is to make the board itself. Using squared timber, Bankan-san makes a frame and then glues plywood onto it. He nails the plywood into place.

2 Next, he paints the whole board evenly with paste.

3 He glues paper onto the board, spreading it out with a large brush to prevent lumps and bubbles forming.

4 Using a poster for reference, Bankan-san draw the outlines of the design with a lead pencil.

5 He paints with *doroenogu*, an opaque, muddy paint used only in Japan.

6 After the color has been applied, he checks the overall look.

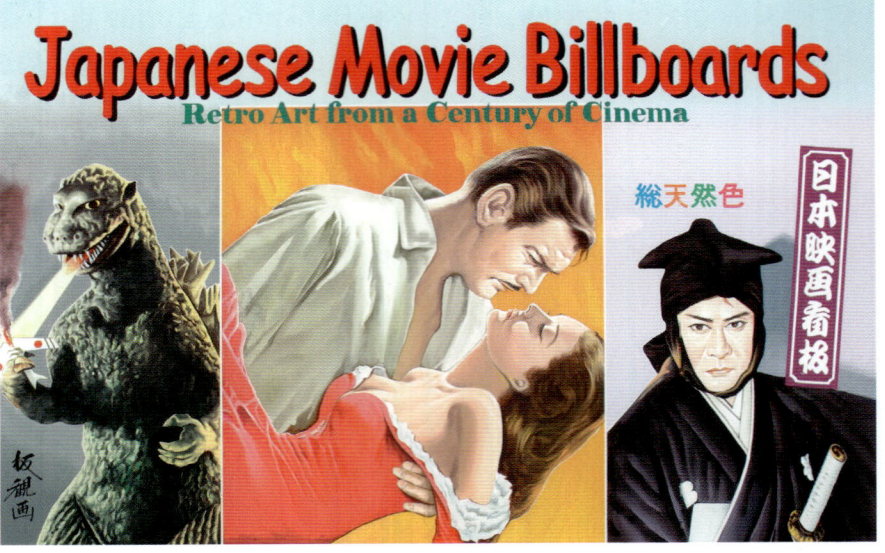

Japanese Movie Billboards
Retro Art from a Century of Cinema

7 To finish, Bankan-san adds lettering, and the billboard is complete.

Tools Used in Billboard Painting

Doroenogu
The five basic colors used are white, yellow, red, blue and black. The colors are mixed to create a variety of other colors.

Brushes
Bankan-san has used the same brushes for a very long time. In order to render various lines and expressions, he uses a variety of brushes.

Nikawa
Nikawa is a glue-like substance made from animal bones and other natural materials. It is melted and mixed with the paint.

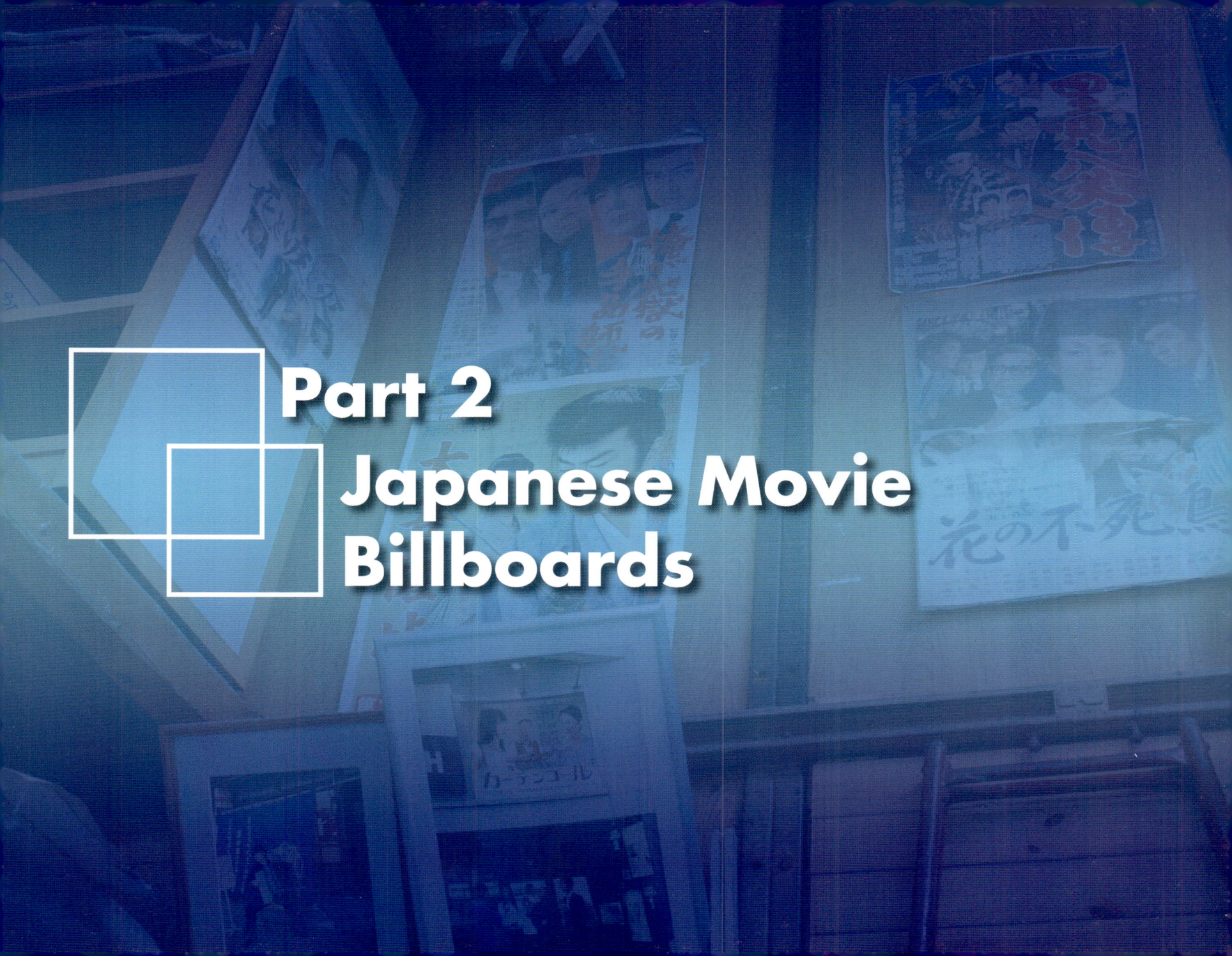

Part 2
Japanese Movie Billboards

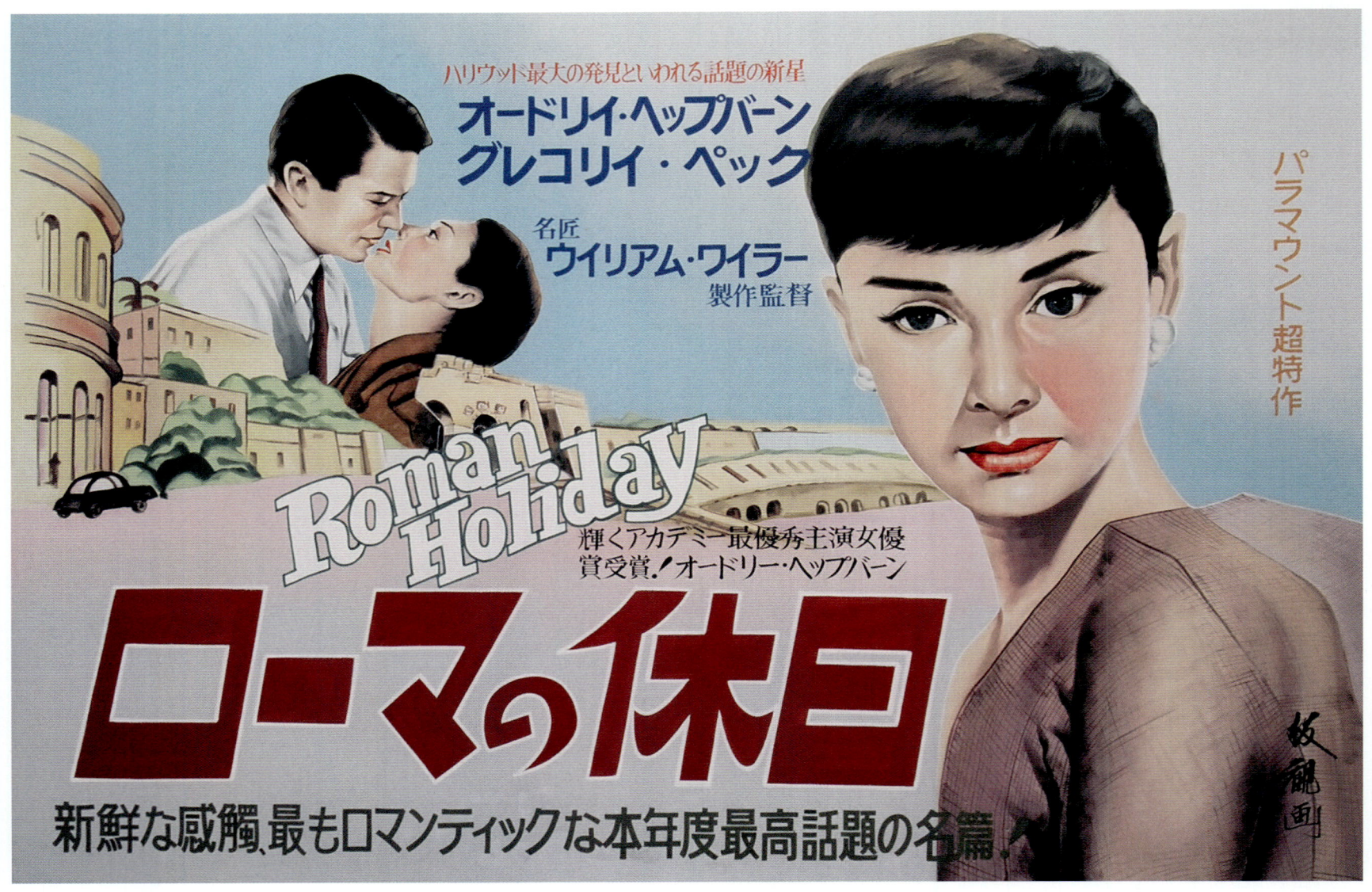

Roman Holiday
It will give you goose bumps! The year's most talked about romantic movie.
U.S.A/1953/William Wyler

Casablanca
Multiple-award winner! The greatest love story in the history of cinema will lift your heart.
U.S.A/1943/Michael Curtiz

The Bodyguard
Japan / 1961 / Akira Kurosawa

Musashi Miyamoto
"I will never be defeated!" is the battle cry of the indomitable Musashi!
Japan/1961/Tomu Utida

Shane
The greatest Western in the history of the movies!
U.S.A/1953/George Stevens

Gone with The Wind
Scarlett O'Hara. She lived for love in the eye of the storm.
U.S.A/1939/Victor Fleming

Purple Hood
The mysterious swordsman Purple Hood rises up against the tempestuous tyrant Tanuma! Chiezou plays four parts in this thrilling masterpiece!
Japan/1959/Hideaki Onisi

New Tales from Many Lands The Flute Playing Boy
There is a witch on Blackhair Mountain! Her underlings, the cheerful monsters are in place and Hagimaru is in danger! Where is Kikyou? Kikumaru, come quickly and bring your flute!
Japan/1954/Ryou Ogiwara

The Seven Samurai
Raiders attack! Seven over-matched samurai boldly take them on in this monumental action picture!
Japan/1954/Akira Kurosawa

Charlie Chaplin in "Police"
Explosive laughter and pathos mingle in this story about a thief who was duped by a crooked priest and chased by a policeman.
U.S.A/1916/Charles Chaplin

Hanabi
Is there anyone out there who will take me in their arms?
Japan/1998/Takesi Kitano

Crimson Wings
Tough guy Yuichirou's fighting spirit and love of humanity straddle heaven and earth in this epic masterpiece!
Japan/1958/Kou Nakahira

The Storm Summoner
Glory is mine! My fists fly wildly in a manic rhythm! Renouncing love, his hot-blooded spirit boils with ambition!
Japan/1957/Umetugu Inoue

Bonnie and Clyde
A brief moment of young love is heartlessly snuffed out with 87 shots.
U.S.A/1967/Arthur Penn

Arch of Triumph
A triumph for Bergman that is a worthy follow-up to Casablanca. Romance comes to life on the drizzly Paris streets on the eve of World War II. Remarque's towering novel has now become a motion picture.
U.S.A/1948/Lewis Milestone

September Affair
Love comes unexpectedly during a lonely jouney... with a love song that will break your heart.
U.S.A/1950/William Dieterle

Happiness and Pain and the Passing of Time
A lyric poem of emotion and tears woven from the fabric of life, past and future.
Japan/1957/Keisuke Kinoshita

Pepe Le Moko
Because of a once-in-a-lifetime love, because of unbearable nostalgia, the villain Pepe gives up his stormy life in a masterpiece by Duvivier and Gabin that surpasses 'La Bandera' and 'La Belle Equipe'.
French/1937/Julien Duvivier

The Town with the Cupola
Pitch black ash falls from the evening sky depicting the hopes and dreams of destitute children. An uplifting declaration of hope from the 'pure love' team!
Japan/1962/Kirio Urayama

La Strada
Floating on the melody of the heartbreaking theme song 'Gelsomina' this never-to-be-forgotten masterpiece sings the praises of immortal love.
French/1954/Federico Fellini

Hibari, Chiemi and Izumi are the Three Sisters
A sweet rainbow of love leaps out of the music.
Japan/1955/Toshio Sugie

Piein Soleil
A dazzling port in southern Italy helps a young man's dreams come to life!
France/1960/Rene Clement

The Man with No Tomorrow
Surviving another day means being faster on the draw! A pistol has no use for emotion! The indomitable Kei'ichirou Akagi has a license to kill.
Japan/1960/Hiroshi Noguchi

Crimson Pistol
The wonder lives on forever! Kei'ichirou Akagi's greatest masterpiece!
Japan/1961/Yoichi Usihara

オードリー・ヘプバーン
ジョージ・ペパード
パトリシア・ニール
監督・ブレイク・エドワーズ

しる珠玉の名篇！

で朝食を

ィファニーの前でささやかな朝食
りの幸せであった……

Breakfast at Tiffany's
The magnificent gem you've been waiting for! A modest breakfast in front of Tiffany's was the happiest moment.
U.S.A/1961/Blake Edwards

The Red Peony Gambler Oryu Comes Calling
If you want to see the red peony under my cloak that badly,
I'll show it to you. But it will cost you your life.
Japan/1970/Tai Katou

Tangesazen The One-armed, One-eyed Ronin The Enchanted Sword "Wet Swallow"
An enraged renegade swordsman with an unquenchable thirst for blood in this lively epic from Ryutarou Otomo!
Japan/1958/Fubo Hayashi

On the Waterfront
A sharply drawn drama set against the background of the swirling violence of the New York waterfront.
U.S.A/1954/Elia Kazan

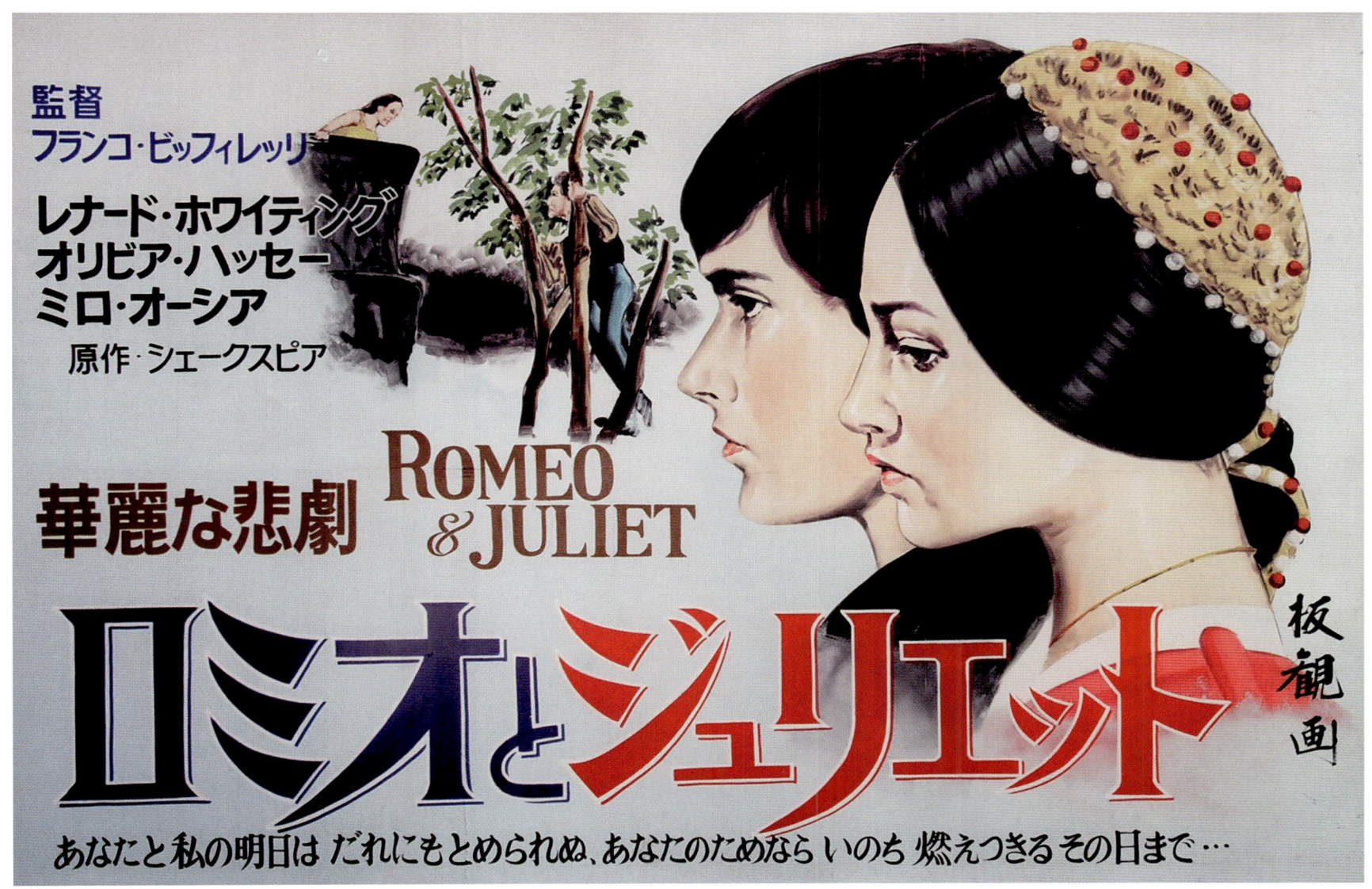

Romeo & Juliet
No one can keep us apart, until the day I die...
UK/1968/Franco Zeffirelli

Some Like it Hot
On the run from some gangsters, two guys stumble into an all-girl paradise. A sophisticated, sexy comedy!
U.S.A/1959/Billy Wilder

Goodbye Milky Way Railroad 999
Two years later, the Milky Way Railroad 999 embarks on its last journey, carrying young love…
Japan/1981/Reiji Matsumoto

The Flavour of Pike
A father's love tries to protect his daughter's happiness when she leaves home to find work.
Japan/1962/Yasujiro Ozu

Wheat Harvest
A chic and stylish cinematic tour de force.
Japan/1951/Yasujiro Odu

Love Story
Love means no regrets!
U.S.A/1970/Arthur Hiller

The Notorious Port
Intensity that will rattle your teeth! The 'Notorious' team show up in a wicked, sexy port.
Japan/1963/Kazuo Mori

Stagecoach
A Western that tells you everything you need to know about the genius of John Ford!
U.S.A/1939/John Ford

The Kid
Cute but mischievous little Jackie Coogan and Charlie Chaplain team up to make you laugh till you cry. This great film reveals Chaplain to be a true genius.
U.S.A/1921/Charles Chaplin

Epic Poem
This magnificent epic portrait of pure love is beautiful, sad, and heart breaking!
Japan/1958/Eisuke Takizawa

The Sound of Music
The sun is shining, the plants are sprouting... a victory song full of happiness and emotion that fills the air.
U.S.A/1965/Robert Wise

She Wore a Yellow Ribbon
John Ford pens a nostalgic ode to the old West!
U.S.A/1949/John Ford

The Summer of the Eclipse
Reacting to the corrupt world of adults, young people searching for pure love find love and heartbreaking pain. Yujirou Ishihara gives a heartfelt portrayal of rebellious youth.
Japan/1956/Hiromichi Horikawa

The Bridge on the River Kwai
The greatest war film ever made, from the team that brought you Lawrence of Arabia.
U.S.A/1957/David Lean

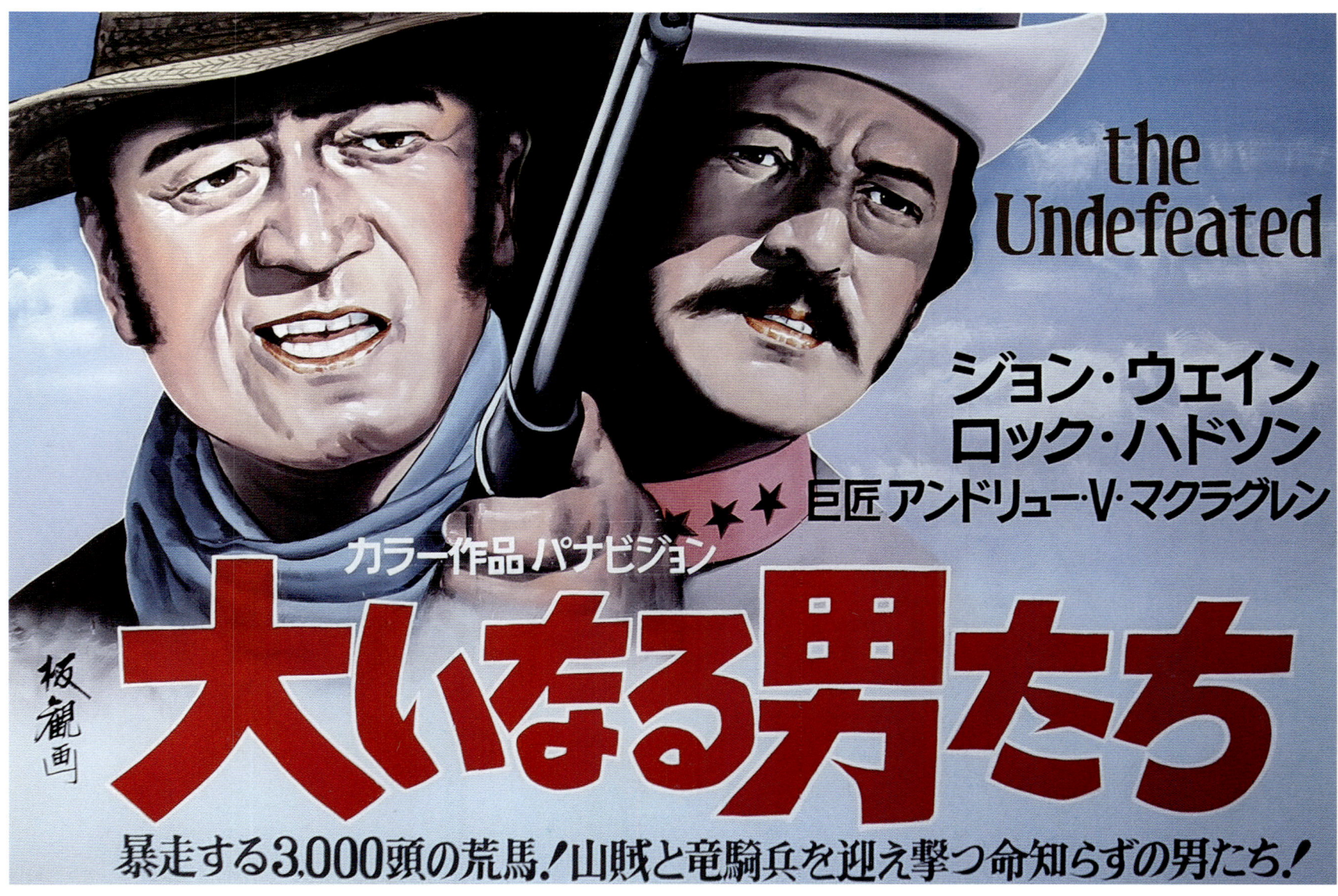

The Undefeated
A stampede of 3,000 wild horses! A bandit and a cavalryman meet head on without fear!
U.S.A/1969/Andrew V McLaglen

Zatoichi The Blind Swordsman Nidangiri
Deprived of sound and smell, will Zatoichi be able to unsheathe his sword
and unleash his new technique, the Nidangiri (double-layer of death)?
Japan / 1965 / Akira Inoue

Teenaged President
The friendship of a globetrotting man and the longing of a woman. Yuujirou, Ruriko, and the Johnnys make the sparks fly in this masterpiece of emotion and music.
Japan/1966/Ezaki Mikio

Princess Mononoke
Live.
Japan/1997/Hyao Miyazaki

Be Forever Yamato
Yamato embarks on a journey without end, into the infinite universe… forever
Japan/1980/Reiji Matsumoto

Shinsengumi
Japan's greatest samurai wield their swords to defend truth and honour against a band of assassins!
Japan/1969/Tadashi Sawashima

Tales of Eight Dogs The Monsters' Ball
Unequalled thrills overflow in the long-awaited sequel to this historical adventure story.
Japan/1959/Kokichi Uchide

High Noon
Two guns break the deathly silence! It's four against one in a sea of blood and sweat.
U.S.A/1952/Fred Zinnemann

It's Tough to be a Man   The Talk about Torajirou
You say I've got no luck with women? I don't need you to tell me that. I'm the one who's suffering, aren't I?
Japan/1978/Yoji Yamada

It's Tough to be a Man   Torajirou's Forget-me-not Grass
You know how sometimes you meet someone and you don't think anything of it until after they're gone? She was that kind of woman.
Japan/1973/Yoji Yamada

It's Tough to be a Man   Torajirou on the Path of Truth
Love hurts this time around, and it's a painful journey to the far-away Path of Truth
Japan/1984/Yoji Yamada

It's Tough to be a Man   Torajirou is Lovesick
I'm not in love, eh? I just want her to be happy, that's all!
Japan/1974/Yoji Yamada

Pacific Porters
Gallop on silver wings! Propellers howl! Akira Kobayashi strides across the sky in this heroic tale!
Japan/1961/Seiji Hoshikawa

Himeyuri's Tower
This film is dedicated to the spirits of the more than 200 members of the Himeyuri Brigade who sacrificed their chaste bodies for the fatherland. This is the beautiful and painful hidden story of the young girls who died nobly in the embrace of war.
Japan/1953/Tadashi Imai

Chisum
Blood rains down on Lincoln County! The hero John Chisum and the outlaw Billy the Kid are trapped by their sterile code of honour in this true story of the old West
U.S.A/1970/Andrew V McLaglen

The Enemy Below
Two men fight a heroic secret battle on the stormy seas of the south Atlantic
U.S.A/1957/Dick Powell

Senhime
A woman lives for love, but love is denied to Senhime — a tragic tale that will make every woman sob.
Japan/1954/Masaichi Nagata

New Tales from Many Lands The Red Peacock
A yearlong series compressed into an hour-long episode for your viewing pleasure.
Japan/1954/Ryou Ogiwara

Texas Across the River
A Comanche tidal wave! A terrifying
moment of truth!
U.S.A/1966/Michael Gordon

Le Notti Di Cabiria
Our lucky day will arrive sometime! The hopes, fears, and good intentions of modern women are expressed through the tragic figure of Caribia. A moving work of limitless poetry and beauty.
Italy/1951/Federico Fellini

The Kurama Goblin The Wandering Child Acrobats
An intensely delightful historical masterpiece full of drama!
Japan/1953/Nobuo Adachi

The Big Boss
A terrible force threatens the Man of Steel!
The whole fascinating story will finally be told!
Hong kong/1971/Lou Way

Dangerous G-Men The Beast of the Underworld
Strikingly strong and glamorous! Shinji Hata emerges as a new star!
Japan/1960/Masamitu Igayama

The Man Who Crossed Hell
A howling storm of flying fists! Singer Shinji Hata's third action film!
Japan/1960/Satoru Sonoda

Lawrence of Arabia
Lawrence leads the Arab nation against the German-Turkish alliance. The soldier of fortune bets his life on the burning sands.
UK/1962/David Lean

The Naked Edge
There were no advance screenings for critics or reporters, in order to keep the ending of this thriller a secret.
UK/1961/Michael Anderson

Nonchan Rides the Clouds
This affectionate masterpiece about childish longing to gather the floating clouds will warm your heart!
Japan/1955/Humindo Kurata

Lonely Iyami in the Wind
Japan/Fujio Akatsuka

Momotarou, the Musical
Japan/Fujio Akatsuka

West Side Story
A ground-breaking musical set in the heart of New York. Beautiful melodies! Dynamic dance numbers! Breath-taking action!
U.S.A/1961/Robert Wise

The Third Man
A devastating battle between hunter and hunted in post-war Vienna. A deft portrait of the deep recesses of a woman's fickle heart and human psychology.
UK/1949/Carol Reed

Your Name Is… Part 3
The final episode in this inspirational story that has the whole country talking!
Japan/1954/Hideo Oba

Abashiri Special Zone Showdown in the South
Full speed ahead to the Higashi Shina Sea. Takakura shows them whose boss in Okinawa!
Japan/1966/Teruo Ishii

Darling Clementine
Finally! A masterful Western worthy of Stagecoach's John Ford.
U.S.A/1946/John Ford

Jeux Interdits
Who stole this little girl's happiness and dreams? Humanism and an unflinching protest against the horror of war fill this work.
France/1952/René Clément

Daibosatsu Ridge Part 2
The Kougen swordsmen lie low and wait coolly for their chance!
Japan/1958/Tomu Utida

Daibosatsu Ridge The Kougen Swordsmen
The sword will cry or blood will laugh in Ryounosuke Tsukue's night of madness!
Japan/1953/Kunio Watanabe

Daibosatsu Ridge The Epilogue
The whole story is wrapped up in this stormy climax!
Japan/1959/Tomu Utida

Floral Phoenix
Love lives on even after you die... An alluring work that sings the praises of a woman's heart, through a score of 14 beloved songs!
Japan/1970/Umeji Inoue

Nakanori, the Bloody Fool!
She sings, she dances, Hibari does it all with verve!
Japan / 1961 / Masamitsu Igayama

Tarzan Escapes
Thrills and laughs in a jungle full of man-eating beasts and cannibals!
U.S.A/1936/Richard Thorpe

City Lights
A single rose blooms on a street corner and turns on the lamp of love! A Chaplin masterpiece full of laughter and tears!
U.S.A/1953/Chales Chaplin

The Great Escape
Three hours of breathless tension! Allied soldiers make a miraculous escape from a high-security Nazi prison camp! The stakes in this great game are life itself!
U.S.A/1953/John Sturges

The Foghorn Calls to Me
The violent passion of the sea and the mournful wail of the foghorn. Kei'ichirou Akagi shows that he has what it takes in a battle on the lawless docks.
Japan/1953/Tokujiro Yamazaki

A short biography of Bankan Kubo

Bankan Kubo was born in Ome City, Tokyo Prefecture, in 1941. After graduating from middle school, he painted hundreds of small-scale movie billboards by copying the originals and made up his mind to make a career of as a movie-billboard artist.

In 1954, he sold his own movie billboards to a local movie theatre called the Ome Dai'ei, launching his career as a young billboard artist. Two years later, he became the exclusive billboard artist of the Ome Kinema and Ome Central movie theatres, painting billboards at a rate of one per day, at his peak.

However, in the 70s, the movie industry went into decline as a result of media such as television and all three of the movie theatres in Ome closed their doors, causing him to lose his job as a billboard artist.

A turning point arrived in 1993, with the advent of the Ome Art Festival, as a result of which Bankan's billboards were publicly displayed on the Ome shopping street for the first time in 19 years.

Movie Billboard Museum • Showa Magic Lantern Hall

Ome City has built three facilities, the Ome Akatsuka Fujio Memorial Hall, the Showa Museum of Retro Products, and the Showa Magic Lantern Hall, as part of its 'Streets of Showa' themed, urban-renewal project. Many of Bankan Kubo's movie billboards are on display in the Showa Magic Lantern Hall. The warm, hand-painted billboards hanging on the wall are now rarities, giving the hall a nostalgic feeling.

This museum also features a diorama of life back in the Showa era.

Hours	10 am to 5 pm
Holidays	The museum is closed on Mondays (or the following day if Monday is a public holiday) and during the year-end holiday period.
Admission	Adults 200 yen, elementary and middle-school students 100 yen
Phone	0428-20-0355

INDEX

A
Abashiri Special Zone Showdown in the South   83
Arch of Triumph   24

B
Be Forever Yamato   56
Bonnie and Clyde   23
Breakfast at Tiffany's   34

C
Casablanca   13
Charlie Chaplin in "Police"   20
Chisum   64
City Lights   91
Crimson Pistol   33
Crimson Wings   22

D
Daibosatsu Ridge Part 2   86
Daibosatsu Ridge The Kougen Swordsmen   87
Daibosatsu Ridge The Epilogue   87
Dangerous G-Men The Beast of the Underworld   72
Darling Clementine   84

E
Epic Poem   47

F
Floral Phoenix   88

G
Gone with The Wind   17
Goodbye Milky Way Railroad 999   41

H
Hanabi   21
Happiness and Pain and the Passing of Time   26
Hibari, Chiemi, and Izumi Are the Three Sisters   31
High Noon   59
Himeyuri's Tower   63

I
It's Tough to be a Man   The Talk about Torajirou   60
It's Tough to be a Man   Torajirou is Lovesick   61
It's Tough to be a Man   Torajirou on the Path of Truth   61
It's Tough to be a Man   Torajirou's Forget-me-not Grass   61

J
Jeux Interdits   85

L
La Strada   30
Lawrence of Arabia   74
Le Notti Di Cabiria   69
Lonely Iyami in the Wind   78
Love Story   43

M
Momotarou, the Musical   79
Movie Billboard Museum · Showa Magic Lantern Hall   95
Musashi Miyamoto   15

N
Nakanori, the Bloody Fool!   89
New Tales from Many Lands The Flute Playing Boy   19
New Tales from Many Lands The Red Peacock   67
Nonchan Rides the Clouds   77

O
On the Waterfront   38

P
Pacific Porters   62
Pepe Le Moko   27
Plein Soleil   32
Princess Mononoke   56
Purple Hood   18

R
Roman Holiday   12
Romeo & Juliet   39

S
Senhime   66
September Affair   25
Shane   16
She Wore a Yellow Ribbon   50
Shinsengumi   57
Some Like it Hot   40
Stagecoach   45

T
Tales of Eight Dogs The Monsters' Ball   58
Tangesazen The One-armed, One-eyed Ronin The Enchanted Sword "Wet Swallow"   37
Tarzan Escapes   90
Teenaged President   55
Texas Across the River   68
The Big Boss   71
The Bodyguard   14
THE Bridge on the River Kwai   52
The Enemy Below   65
The Flavour of Pike   42
The Foghorn Calls to Me   93
The Great Escape   92
The Kid   46
The Kurama Goblin The Wandering Child Acrobats   70
The Man Who Crossed Hell   73
The Man with No Tomorrow   33
The Naked Edge   76
The Notorious Port   44
The Red Peony Gambler Oryu Comes Calling   36
The Seven Samurai   20
The Sound of Music   48
The Storm Summoner   22
The Summer of the Eclipse   51
The Third Man   81
The Town with the Cupola   28
The Undefeated   53

W
West Side Story   80
Wheat Harvest   42

Y
Your Name Is... Part 3   82

Z
Zatoichi The Blind Swordsman Nidangiri   54

Japanese Movie Billboards

Thank you for choosing this book. DH Publishing specializes in books on Japanese pop and underground cultures. Check out what's new on our website and register to receive updates live from Tokyo.

www.dhp-online.com

...of otaku, by otaku, for otaku...